Watch it Grow

A Bean's Life

Nancy Dickmann

www.raintreepublishers.co.uk

Visit our website to find out more information about Raintree books.

To order:

☎ Phone 0845 6044371

▤ Fax +44 (0) 1865 312263

▧ Email myorders@raintreepublishers.co.uk

Customers from outside the UK please telephone +44 1865 312262

Raintree is an imprint of Capstone Global Library Limited, a company incorporated in England and Wales having its registered office at 7 Pilgrim Street, London, EC4V 6LB – Registered company number: 6695582

Text © Capstone Global Library Limited 2010
First published in hardback in 2010
The moral rights of the proprietor have been asserted.

Edited by Nancy Dickmann, Rebecca Rissman, and Catherine Veitch
Designed by Joanna Hinton-Malivoire
Picture research by Mica Brancic
Production by Victoria Fitzgerald
Originated by Capstone Global Library Ltd
Printed and bound in China by South China Printing Company Ltd

ISBN 978 0 431 19538 4
14 13 12 11 10
10 9 8 7 6 5 4 3 2

British Library Cataloguing in Publication Data
Dickmann, Nancy.
Bean. -- (Watch it grow)
583.7'4-dc22

Acknowledgements

We would would like to thank the following for permission to reproduce photographs: Corbis pp. **4** (Flame/© Tim Pannell), **7** (© Gary K Smith), **12** (Photoconcepts/© Bill Holden); FLPA p. **13** (© Gary K Smith); Getty Images p. **19** (FoodPix/Sandra Ivany); iStockphoto pp. **6** (© quidnunc), **10** (redmal), **18** (floortje), **20** (RawFile), **22 top** (© quidnunc), **22 left** (floortje), **22 right** (redmal), **23 top** (floortje), **23 middle top** (Arlindo 71), **23 bottom** (redmal); Nature Picture Library p. **17** (© Adam White); Photolibrary pp. **5** (Flirt Collection/Corbis), **8** (Imagestate RM/© Gary Smith), **9** (© Oxford Scientific (OSF)), **14** (Garden Picture Library/© Maxine Adcock), **15** (Garden Picture Library/© Howard Rice), **21** (© Oxford Scientific (OSF)), **22 bottom** (Garden Picture Library/© Howard Rice), **23 middle bottom** (© Oxford Scientific (OSF)); Shutterstock p. **11** (Marek Pawluczuk); **16** (Jo Stafford).

Front cover photograph (main) of harvested broad beans reproduced with permission of iStockphoto (© Frederique Catherine Jones). Front cover photograph (inset) of bean shoots reproduced with permission of Shutterstock (© Filipe B. Varela). Back cover photograph of a bean shoot reproduced with permission of iStockphoto (redmal).

The publisher would like to thank Nancy Harris for her assistance in the preparation of this book.

Contents

Life cycles

All living things have a life cycle.

A bean has a life cycle.

A bean is a seed. It grows into a new bean plant.

The bean plant grows beans.
Later it will die.

Seeds and shoots

A bean grows in the ground.

root

Roots grow down from the seed into the ground.

shoot

A shoot grows from the bean.

leaves

Leaves grow from the shoot.

Becoming a bean plant

The bean plant needs water and sunlight to grow.

The bean plant grows bigger.

The bean plant grows flowers in
the spring.

flower

The flowers are white with dark spots.

Making seeds

A bee comes to feed on a flower.

The bee has pollen on it.

new bean

The pollen helps make new beans
grow on the plant.

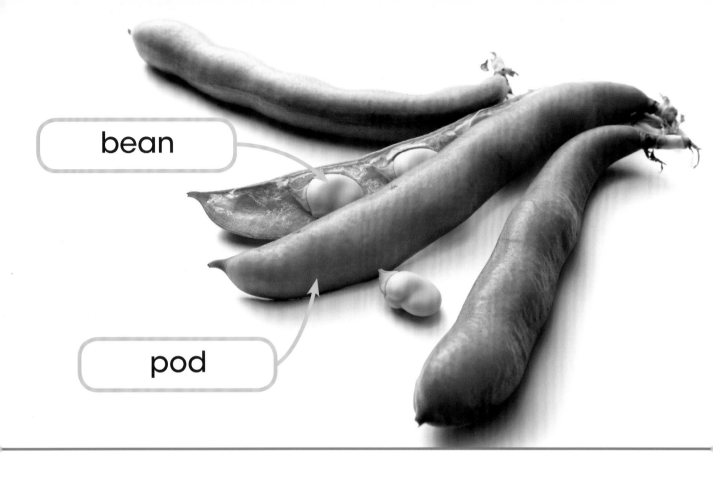

bean

pod

The beans grow inside a pod.

The pods look lumpy when the
beans are grown.

Some beans fall to the ground.

The life cycle starts again.

Life cycle of a bean plant

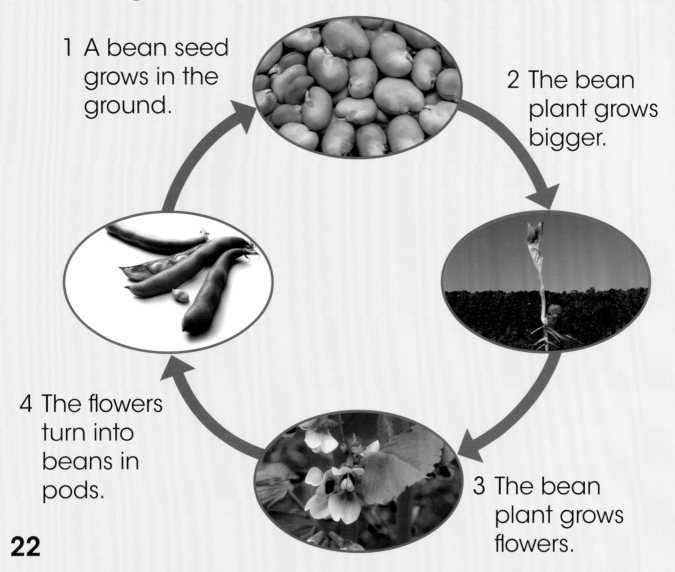

1 A bean seed grows in the ground.

2 The bean plant grows bigger.

4 The flowers turn into beans in pods.

3 The bean plant grows flowers.

22

Picture glossary

pod tough outer case that protects seeds such as beans

pollen yellow powder inside a flower

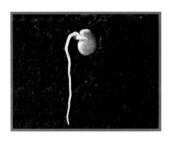

root part of a plant that grows underground. Roots take up water for the plant to use.

shoot small green stem that grows from a seed

Index

Notes to parents and teachers
Before reading
Show the children a broad bean pod and ask if they know what's inside. Hand out some pods and get them to open them up and look at the beans. Ask the children if they have ever grown beans. Do they like to eat them?

After reading
• Give each child an empty yogurt pot, some soil and a broad bean to plant. Make sure they keep their pots in sunlight and water the growing plants regularly. If your school has a garden, move the plants outside when they are big enough.

• Do some broad bean maths together. Collect some broad bean pods and measure them. How long is the biggest pod? How long is the smallest? Can the children guess how many beans are in each pod? Open up the pods and count the number of beans. Are there more beans in the longest pod?

• Read Jim and the Beanstalk by Raymond Briggs.